PENN

IN OLD PHOTOGRAPHS

PENN

IN OLD PHOTOGRAPHS

————————COLLECTED BY————————
ELIZABETH A. REES

ALAN SUTTON

Alan Sutton Publishing Limited
Phoenix Mill · Far Thrupp · Stroud · Gloucestershire

First published 1990

British Library Cataloguing in Publication Data

Penn in old Photographs.
1. West Midlands (Metropolitan County). Wolverhampton.
Penn, history
I. Rees, Elizabeth
942.491

ISBN 0–86299–715–1

Typeset in 9/10 Korinna.
Typesetting and origination by
Alan Sutton Publishing Limited.
Printed in Great Britain by
Dotesios Printers Limited.

CONTENTS

INTRODUCTION

Penn, a former village now mainly within the borough of Wolverhampton, had its origins in pre-Saxon times and the name is a British one meaning 'hill'. Even today it is obvious that the nucleus of the village, around St Bartholomew's church, stands at the top of a hill – Church Hill on one side, and the land that falls away as Penn Common on the other.

It is at the top of this hill that the only remnant of early Penn may still be found – the base of the Saxon preaching cross in the churchyard of St Bartholomew's. At this time Penn was under the lordship of the famous Lady Godiva and her son Earl Aelfgar. The earliest documentary mention of Penn may date from the year 994. The charter by which Lady Wulfrun gave her land to the church at Wolverhampton mentions the Penwie or Penn Way, a route which possibly linked Bushbury with Penn. The same charter mentions the Goldhoard, thought to be an early form of Goldthorn.

By the time of the Domesday Survey in 1086 Penn was a small settlement. The land was held by the Norman William FitzAnsculf, the lord of Dudley who had acquired it from the pre-Conquest Mercian owners, probably in 1071. There were fourteen villeins, one freeman and two bordars, all with their families, perhaps just over a hundred people in total, actually living there.

In about 1200 the parish church, which may then have been dedicated to John the Baptist, and was almost certainly on the site of an earlier religious centre, was founded. At about the same time the estate of Trescott Grange, one of the most important properties in the Lower Penn area, was given to the monks of Combe Abbey, Warwickshire. The parish of Penn was divided into a number of hamlets, which remained physically separate until the nineteenth century. These included Upper Penn, Lower Penn, Muchall, Merry Hill, Bradmore and Finchfield. By the sixteenth century, the population of the parish had increased to perhaps 300 people, scattered over a wide area.

A century later Penn was a relatively prosperous village. A few houses and cottages still survive from this period showing that at least some of the people could afford to live in substantial dwellings. Some could also afford to leave money for the support of the poorer members of the community, the earliest example being Alice Green, who in 1606 left ten shillings annually, chargeable on a farm in Sedgley. In 1659 Roger Baker left two farms called Bradmore and Beckmaster for the support of eighteen poor people. More famously, in 1669 Charles Winn, vicar of Penn from 1646, left money to found a school and to buy Bibles for local children on their leaving the school. This charity, and the school which opened in 1714, are still in existence, as are the five almshouses in Pennwood Lane left by Raphael and Anne Sedgwick in 1747. They had also built Penn Hall as a hospital, according to Stebbing Shaw the eighteenth-century historian, but it was never used as one. The parishioners also had sufficient surplus at this time to embark on a substantial rebuilding of the church, the brick tower of which still remains more or less as they left it. The old tower had been of sandstone which had probably weathered over the centuries.

Life for most people in Penn was based on agriculture. Many eighteenth-century farmhouses, which were working farms right up until the middle years of this century, still survive around the parish, although now converted into private houses. There was, however, some industrial activity. Furnace Grange was the site of early iron smelting, Baggeridge on the borders of Penn Common provided coal and clay for bricks, and there were gravel pits at Muchall, near the Stag's Head, and on the Penn Road. Some Penn people, like those of neighbouring Sedgley, also carried out work such as nailmaking at home, and Bradmore was famous for its gunlocks.

In the eighteenth century Penn Road was made into a turnpike road with toll-gates at Stubbs Lane/Coalway Lane and near where the orphanage was later to be built. Local traffic could avoid these tolls, however, by sticking to the old tracks across the Common and the farmlands between Penn and Wolverhampton.

In 1830 the population of Upper Penn was still only about 700 but by 1871 this had increased to nearly 1,900, with a further increase of 600 over the next 10 years. Lower Penn in 1881 had a further 335 people, but had remained fairly static, and actually decreased by 1891. Lower Penn did not increase markedly in population until the 1950s and then largely because of building in the Springhill and Showell Lane areas. Most of the parish has remained rural in character.

By the nineteenth century the Penn Road and Penn village were also becoming favoured residences for wealthy industrialists and professional men from Wolverhampton, along with their families and households of servants. Among those who chose Penn were Henry Beckett, surveyor; Sidney Cartwright JP, Charles Clarke, carriage builder; Randle Shaw Walker, surveyor; William Henry Rogers, merchant; Thomas Moss Phillips, solicitor and industrialist, as well as various members of the Sparrow, Twentyman and Mander families. The wealthiest bought up the old mansions of Penn itself while others built their own villas closer to the town. By the end of the First World War Penn Road was almost completely built up as far as the Beeches on the far side of Penn village.

The early years of the twentieth century saw huge changes in the history of Penn. Firstly, as happened elsewhere in Britain, the large estates began to be broken up. The huge Lloyd Estate was auctioned off in 1901, and while most of the farms at that time remained intact and working, this opened the way for the later cutting of new streets and building of houses. At the same time, the population of Wolverhampton was growing and, more importantly, seeking to move to better quality areas outside the town centre.

Penn Fields was the first district to become effectively part of Wolverhampton's urban area. By the mid-nineteenth century it was sufficiently populous to become a parish in its own right with the building of St Philip's church, but later in the century its focus moved from the area close to Coalway Road and the church to Lea Road where numerous streets of terraced houses were completed by speculative builders in the Edwardian period. Services such as shops, pubs, schools and churches naturally accompanied this growth. Birches Barn and the Beckminster estate remained open land a little longer, but were selected for the site of Wolverhampton's first municipal housing under the 'homes for heroes' scheme after the First World War. On the Birches Barn estate 396 houses were built, and a further 216 at Beckminster before the rest of this estate was sold off for private housing.

The inter-war years in general saw a building boom and private houses sprang up in the Penn area, particularly in Coalway Road, Oxbarn and St Philip's Avenue in the 1920s. The Penn Court, Penn House and Woodlands estates were all laid out as building land in the mid-1930s. Council house building also continued with a huge estate at Warstones in the 1930s. In 1933 Upper Penn became administratively part of the borough of Wolverhampton.

Meanwhile, Penn Common had become something of a recreational area. Outings to the Common were popular and became easier as bus and tram services from Wolverhampton expanded. In the early years of the nineteenth century there was a racecourse on the Common. Here it was not only possible to watch the races but also to enjoy other pursuits such as bare-fist pugilism which were illegal within the boundaries of Wolverhampton. Even after the disappearance of this organized entertainment the Common was popular with walkers and picnickers and a number of pubs and tea shops catered for them. From 1892 golf was available to members of the club and small boys could enjoy themselves chasing after the balls. During the Second World War anti-aircraft guns were positioned on the Common and American servicemen billeted there. Wartime secrecy has meant that these have left little trace in the written record but they are well remembered by local residents.

Since the war the Common has once again become a peaceful tract of open land and is now protected as part of the Green Belt, as is Lower Penn. Elsewhere housing development has continued unabated and Upper Penn is now very much a part of Wolverhampton and the West Midlands conurbation. Older residents regret the passing of the village life that they knew until comparatively recently, but there is no doubt that Penn is still seen as a desirable part of the town in which to live, and many of the physical vestiges of the past still survive.

Around Penn Village

LLOYD FARM, LLOYD HILL C. 1900. The farmer at this time was Neil Ferguson who was also a corn factor in Wombourne. From the state of the road surface this was obviously a busy route even in those days.

TWO PHOTOGRAPHS OF CHURCH HILL, taken in winter and summer respectively, from the junction of Wakeley Hill, showing the house known as the Castle on the right of the road. The oak tree on the green apparently once bore a plaque commemorating Queen Victoria's Jubilee, but this has long since disappeared.

CHURCH HILL looking up from the junction of Wakeley Hill. On the right is the Crofts while on the left, further up the hill is Manor Farm. Horses from this farm would be sent down to the forge on the Penn Road for shoeing, and reputedly find their own way back when turned out afterwards. This of course was in the days before motor traffic became common on the Penn Road. Manor Farm was owned by the Chidlow family and was sold off for housing land in the 1940s.

THE COTTAGE OPPOSITE THE GREEN, CHURCH HILL, photographed in 1894. In the doorway is Mrs T. Sutton and her two daughters. The cottage has now been modernized but still exists.

THE CASTLE, CHURCH HILL. In the last century this was the home of James Lakin who gave the house its castellated appearance. He was well known in Penn as the owner of gravel pits at Colton Hills and a Commoner, and also as the Chairman of Penn Parish Council and a Staffordshire County Councillor. The adjoining building later became a shop.

CHURCH HILL at the junction of Wakeley Hill.

Penn. Nr Wolverhampton.   Copyright.

A POSTCARD VIEW OF PENN, the corner of Church Hill and Pennwood Lane.

MOUNT FARM, PENNWOOD LANE, in 1901 when it was sold to Frank Howard Jeavons for £1,750. It was previously part of the Lloyd Estate.

HORSES were kept by private owners at Mount Farm. This may have been the local doctor, possibly Doctor Spackman.

HAYMAKING AT MOUNT FARM in the 1930s. Mr Price the farmer is third from the right.

MR PRICE PLOUGHING off Pennwood Lane in the 1930s.

HARVESTING OFF PENNWOOD LANE in 1937. In charge of the harvester is Mr Price, while his son and the son of the farm-owner ride the horses.

THE FROZEN POOL, CORNFIELDS WALK. This pool used to freeze over regularly in the winter and was popular with playing children. The ice was never thick, however, and the pool was the scene of more than one tragedy.

ST CATHERINE'S CONVALESCENT HOME in about 1910. Founded as a cottage home for children in 1873, it was given to the Wolverhampton & South Staffordshire General Hospital as a convalescent home for women and children in 1885. Patients had to obtain tickets from subscribers and pay a shilling a week. In 1938 the hospital moved from its orignal site, near where St Catherine's Crescent is now, to the Beeches on Penn Road.

TWO VIEWS OF THE AVENUE.

MAJOR THEODORE ADDENBROOKE lived at Pennover, Vicarage Road. He was an officer of the Boys' Brigade first in Wolverhampton then in Penn for 37 years, until his death in 1931, when 340 boys marched in procession from Mount Road to the graveside. The Penn Boys' Brigade was founded in 1913. Major Addenbrooke was a director of Butler's Brewery in Wolverhampton, and the brewery's delivery lorries served to take the Penn boys to camp at Patshull Park.

MEN OF PENN possibly photographed at one of the large local houses. These include C. Slaten, Harry Higgs and Sam Ford, J. Higgs, H. Price, and William Broome, the organist and choirmaster.

PENN HALL which was completed by Thomas Bradney, high sheriff of Staffordshire in 1752, having been previously designed by Raphael and Anne Sedgwick as a hospital. Among later occupants was John W. Sparrow, the industrialist who was living there in 1851. After falling from private ownership in 1947 it has at various times been a home for nurses and the police, but is now the residential part of Penn Hall Special School, opened in 1974.

MUCHALL MANOR FARM in 1901. This six-bedroomed farmhouse was sold for £2,850 at the break-up of the Lloyd Estate in that year.

COTTAGES OFF PENN ROAD adjoining the Fox & Goose. This close contains some of the oldest houses in Penn.

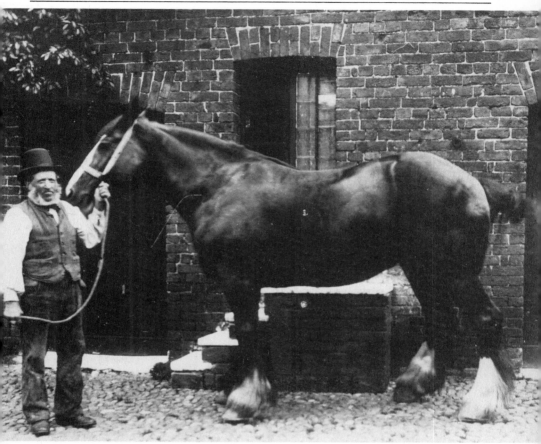

THE PENN BLACKSMITH, MR HENRY RODEN. The forge at this time was in the close adjoining the Fox & Goose, but he later moved to the Penn Road itself where his son Tom followed in his footsteps. The old forge was taken over by Tom Hinsull who ran a coal business. The Roden family was very influential in Penn. Joseph Roden was parish clerk, while Henry Roden took a number of early photographs of the village.

A COTTAGE which probably stood at the Penn Road end of Rookery Lane.

MUCHALL GROVE, pictured in 1908, when it was the home of the Thompson family. The house was purchased by Wolverhampton Borough Council in 1945 and became a civil defence establishment. In 1962 it was decided to use the grounds to build a new old people's home and the original house was demolished around this time.

WAKELEY HILL, formerly called Workhouse Lane, pictured in the 1950s. The upper picture looks down the hill towards Church Hill, with older houses on the right-hand side of the road. The houses on the left were 1930s additions. The lower picture, taken from Church Hill, shows the Fold on the left.

WAKELEY HILL under snow.

THE OLD COTTAGES AT THE CORNER OF MANOR ROAD AND PENN ROAD which were demolished in the 1960s when Penn Road was widened. The top picture shows a flood in 1927.

LLOYD HOUSE, around the 1870s. It was probably built in the late eighteenth century by John Marsh whose descendant married Revd Prebendary William Dalton, first vicar of St Paul's church, Wolverhampton, and founder of St Philip's church, Penn Fields. During his period in the house he held gatherings of local religious men known as the Lloyd Clerical Meetings. The Lloyd Estate was one of the oldest in Penn, the name occurring in Anglo-Saxon charters as *Lude*. It was also one of the largest local landholdings until it was sold off and broken up in 1901.

EARLSWOOD, probably built by Thomas Moss Phillips, a Wolverhampton solicitor, in the early 1860s. His wife Ellen Persehouse Phillips was tragically killed there in 1863 when her dress caught fire and she was badly burned. Following Thomas Moss Phillips' death in 1877 the estate was sold to industrialist George Benjamin Wright and has passed through a number of owners since. It is now used by the 2nd Penn Scouts.

SECTION TWO

Penn Road

PENN ROAD in the early years of the century. The tower of St Peter's church can be seen in the background.

PENN ROAD on a summer day in the 1900s.

THESE TWO PHOTOGRAPHS TAKEN IN PENN VILLAGE in the 1960s illustrate how congested Penn Road had become by this time and how necessary the dual carriageway was which was subsequently provided. The trolleybuses had their own particular difficulties in negotiating parked cars, while a Ministry of Transport survey in 1965 showed that at Lloyd Hill it was the most overloaded trunk road in the country.

CONGESTION IN PENN ROAD.

THE ROSE & CROWN INN, PENN ROAD in the early part of this century. The old inn was rebuilt in the mid-1930s but was again demolished in 1980 after subsidence had made it unsafe. A new Rose & Crown has subsequently been built on the site. In the foreground of the picture, on the opposite side of Church Hill from the pub, was the parish pound. The ladies appear to be looking over the gate at some horses inside.

THE ROSE & CROWN INN in about 1905. Sampson Tharme's horse-drawn bus from Wolverhamtpon, with its conductor standing at the side, can be seen on the right of the picture. This service operated five times daily from 1882 to 1911 and used a team of three horses, probably necessary to haul the vehicle up Swan Bank.

GRAISELEY HILL at about the turn of the century. The temple-like building was the lodge to Graiseley House, home of the Stevens family of AJS motor cycles fame.

PENN ROAD looking back towards the Rose and Crown on a wintry day at the turn of the century. The gateway is that of the Beeches, now the Penn Hospital.

TWO PHOTOGRAPHS SHOWING THE PREMISES OF T.J. NASH, cab proprietor, at the junction of Penn Road and Coalway Road, taken around the 1890s.

THE PREMISES OF T. J. NASH.

THE *WULFRUNA* HORSE-BUS on Penn Road. The road leading off behind the bus is probably the Avenue.

THE PENN ROAD TOLL-GATE, which was near the junction with Coalway Road. Tolls for use of the road were abolished in 1877.

PENN ROAD at the junction with Muchall Road.

DEMOLITION OF THE STRAW HALL, PENN ROAD. This was close to the Royal Orphanage. One story tells of how the owner of this house was robbed and murdered by highwaymen just as he was approaching home, and his body thrown into a sandpit opposite. Early maps of the area show a number of sand and gravel pits in the area, and the fact that one in front of Goldthorn Terrace has never been built on has given rise to the local myth that it is a plague burial pit.

TED AND REG PARNWELL AT HOLLY BUSH COTTAGE C. 1929. These cottages are on the Penn Road opposite the Hollybush Inn, and were also known as Penn Hall Cottages.

THE LEYLANDS in the 1930s. This house still exists but is difficult to see from the road because of the trees which have subsequently grown in front of it.

AN ARCH OF COAL erected across the Penn Road for Queen Victoria's visit to Wolverhampton in November 1866, to unveil the statue of Prince Albert in Queen Square.

TWO VIEWS OF PENN SOME THIRTY YEARS APART showing the police station and the post office. The top picture was taken in the 1900s when the postmistress was Miss Maud Hughes. By the 1930s the post office had acquired a picture window and horses have begun to be replaced by motor transport. The trolleybus poles and wires are also a conspicuous feature.

TWO VIEWS IN THE OPPOSITE DIRECTION after a slightly longer interval of time. The lower postcard picture was taken in the 1950s. The railings outside the shops had been taken for the war effort.

PENN SMITHY, built by Henry Roden and later worked by his two sons Tom and Arthur. Tom was a blacksmith, while Arthur was a carpenter, and together they traded as A. and T. Roden, blacksmiths, wheelwrights and undertakers.

TOM RODEN at work in the smithy in the early 1950s.

TOM AND ARTHUR RODEN working on a wheel in the yard of the smithy. Another rim can be seen in the foreground of the picture surrounded by wood for the fire.

MOUNT ROAD in the 1950s, looking into Belmont Road. The post office had moved from Penn Road by this time.

THE MIDLAND COUNTIES DAIRY at the junction of Penn Road and Lea Road. The dairy was built in typical modernist style in the late 1930s. It was largely a shell enclosing a yard where the machinery for cleaning and filling the milk bottles could be seen through the large windows. Amidst controversy the building was demolished in the late 1980s and has now been replaced by a McDonalds drive-in restaurant.

THE CORNER OF PENN ROAD AND CHURCH HILL in the 1940s.

SECTION THREE

Penn Fields and Bradmore

PENN FIELDS near St Philip's church in the early years of this century. This is probably Coalway Road.

OWEN ROAD in the 1930s. St Chad's church is on the right of the picture.

DUKE STREET in the 1920s.

GOLDTHORN HILL from the junction of Penn Road in the 1900s. The wall on the left is that of Coton House.

"KYBER PASS"
LEA ROAD 1895

LEA ROAD in 1895. This section where the street narrowed was known colloquially as the Khyber Pass. The building on the left stood in front of the Lear Tin Plate Works and was pulled down a few years later. On the right are some brand new houses and the high back wall of the Mount, now the Adult Education Centre, on Penn Road.

A HOUSE AT BRADMORE constructed from an old railway carriage, pictured at about the turn of the century. The carriage is of a very old type, which originally contained six compartments. As the first floor of the house it had been converted into three bedrooms.

LOOKING UP CHURCH ROAD TOWARDS ST PHILIP'S CHURCH in the early years of this century. The little girl is standing at the junction of Coalway Road and the footpath which now leads to Osborne Road. This was formerly the road to Coalway Farm.

TREES IN BIRCHES BARN ROAD in 1908. This road was the old boundary between the parishes of Penn and Wolverhampton.

BECKMINSTER HOUSE, BIRCHES BARN ROAD, built by John William Sparrow in the 1850s. The Sparrow family were industrialists with interests in coal and ironworks in the Bilston area, and another branch of the family lived at Penn Court. Beckminster House, having long been the Wolverhampton Teachers' Centre is now the Education Department Professional Development Centre.

BIRCHES BARN FARMHOUSE. Until the building of the housing estate in the 1920s this was the only building on this side of Birches Barn Road, then known as Birches Barn Lane. At that time the farmer was James Chadwick.

BRADMORE ROAD AND THE BRADMORE INN in the 1920s. The public house now stands on the opposite side of the road, on the site of the houses at the centre of the picture. On the left was the Bradmore Methodist chapel, now the Community Centre.

ST PHILIP'S AVENUE, PENN FIELDS pictured in the 1930s. The arrow points into Beckminster Road, presumably the home of the senders of the postcard.

PENN FIELDS WAR MEMORIAL, engraved 'This statue is erected as a lasting tribute to the men of Penn Fields, Bradmore and Merry Hill who served in His Majesty's forces during the Great War 1914–1919'. Thirty-nine names are also engraved including that of Douglas Morris Harris, a wireless operator who was killed at the age of nineteen while heroically continuing to record messages on board the Italian ship *Floandi*. His individual memorial can be seen in St Peter's Gardens, Wolverhampton.

STUBBS ROAD, PENN FIELDS in about 1907. Because of the difficulties of operating trams on this route, a motorbus service was inaugurated in 1905 making Wolverhampton the first municipal tramways undertaking in Britain to operate a bus service. This operated until the construction of the tram route in 1909.

A LORAIN SYSTEM TRAM at the Penn Fields terminus at the junction of Stubbs Road and Penn Road. Among those pictured on the opening day of the Penn Fields service on 10 September 1909 are Ernie Williams, the conductor; C. Owen Silvers, the Wolverhampton Corporation Transport Manager; Chief Inspector Fred McDonough; Ernie Jeavons, the driver, and Alderman Theodore Mander.

THE CRATER LEFT BY THE BOMB dropped on Beckminster Special School on 3 October 1940. Residents of Penn recall seeing the aircraft which carried out this raid flying low over the area immediately before the bomb fell. It was probably jettisoned to lighten the plane rather than as a deliberate attack.

SECTION FOUR

Penn Common

THE VIEW ACROSS TO SEDGLEY FROM PENN COMMON. The Common remains an important tract of open land within the area in spite of numerous disputes over the past century about its use and ownership. One such in 1912 gave rise to an enquiry in the High Court, the transcribed evidence of which gives us a great deal of information about Penn at that time, as the witnesses could remember it from their childhood.

PENN COMMON at about the turn of the century. On the left of the picture is the Turf Tavern, which still exists although no longer as a pub. The row of cottages is known as Turf Cottages.

THE LLOYD BROOK. This is mentioned as one of the boundaries of Wulfrun's charter of 994 to the church at Wolverhampton, and is thus one of the oldest recorded place-names in the Penn area.

GYPSIES ON PENN COMMON in the last century. It was one of their regular halting places and some residents of Penn still remember the old-fashioned gaily-painted wagons.

NASH'S FARM in about 1905. This part of the Common was quite heavily wooded, in contrast to the section nearer the village.

PENN COMMON IN WINTER, photographed in 1900. The building is possibly Nash's Farm.

SECTION FIVE

Lower Penn

THE GREYHOUND INN, LOWER PENN, with adjoining thatched cottage in 1901. The pub landlord at that time was Benjamin Ives. The Greyhound is already listed as a pub on the Penn tithe map of 1839 and as it has an inscribed stone above the door reading 'WPB 1830' it is possible that it was purpose-built at that time.

PEAR TREE FARM, GREYHOUND LANE, LOWER PENN in 1901 when it was described as a 'compact and convenient farmhouse, substantially built, and containing two bedrooms with fireplaces and two other bedrooms, parlour, kitchen, scullery with bread oven, copper sink etc. and granary over.' The selling price was £970. Above the doorway of the farmhouse is an inscribed stone reading 'E P 1821'. Later this was one of a number of farms worked by the Reed family.

LOWER PENN FARM in 1901.

LANGLEY HALL FARM, LOWER PENN in 1901. The sale catalogue of the Lloyd Estate, of which this farm formed a part, stated that it 'would make a most desirable small pleasure farm, as it is within a short drive of Wolverhampton, in a pretty and elevated situation, and from its position and surroundings should increase in value.'

Merry Hill, Warstones and Springhill

TWO VIEWS OF NEW HOUSE FARM; above in 1901, when the farmer was Joseph Proctor, and below about forty years later, by which time it was known as Warstones Farm. The building itself has hardly changed.

COALWAY ROAD about 1910 when it was still known as Coalway Lane. Although it was widened to twelve yards in 1860 this road did not become built up until the 1920s when a large number of villas were erected within a few years. The name may originate from the fact that this was the way coal was carried from Parkfields, first to the small furnaces on the Smestow and later to the canal.

CASTLECROFT FARM pictured in 1931 when it was sold as 'a highly desirable dairy farm'. The farm formed part of the Castlecroft Estate belonging to Castlecroft House, probably built by Joseph Tarratt in the late eighteenth century, and later the home of the Twentyman family.

ENVILLE ROAD, WARSTONES, shortly after completion in 1949.

A BALLOON FLIES OVER LANGLEY ROAD during the Second World War. It was probably associated with the military camp close by.

HIGHFIELDS FARM, which was farmed by the Collins family. Highfields School now stands on this site.

HARVESTING AT HIGHFIELDS FARM in the 1940s.

A BREAK IN WORK AT HIGHFIELDS FARM in 1942. The machine is a threshing box which was driven by a steam traction engine.

FINE SPECIMENS OF CATTLE AT HIGHFIELDS FARM.

SPRINGHILL in the late 1930s. This parade of shops was built in 1935 and the post office opened in 1936.

THE OFF-LICENCE IN RAYLEIGH ROAD in 1930. The manager is Mr A.J. Poole. Butler's magazine comments that this is 'the usual display and not a special arrangement for the photographer'.

THE STAR STORES at the corner of Trysull Road and Star Street in 1955.

SECTION SEVEN
Social Life in Penn

THE BARLEY MOW INN, PENN COMMON in the early 1920s. This inn is shown on the Penn tithe map of 1840 when one William Powell was the tenant. Its name is a reminder of the malt and barley trade which formerly took place on the Common. Its most well-known landlord was William Lloyd Roberts, tenant from 1891 to 1896 and builder of the tenements which still bear his name on the Common. He was also first steward of the golf club.

THE GUNMAKERS ARMS, TRYSULL ROAD in 1913. It was rebuilt in the 1920s and now occupies the whole of the corner site. Bradmore was a centre of the gunmaking industry from which the pub derives its name.

THE BRUFORD ARMS, PENN FIELDS in 1932. This pub was originally opened as an off-licence in 1910 but was altered and reopened as a pub in 1927. Pictured behind the bar is the landlord Mr Starkey. The exterior photograph is also interesting for the two delivery vehicles parked outside – one selling milk by the can from a churn, and the other selling fresh fish.

THE SPRINGHILL, exterior and interior in 1938 soon after its opening. The pub was designed by local architects Lavender & Twentyman in brick with stone dressings. The rather Spartan interior is in marked contrast to today's pubs.

PENN GOLF CLUB which began in 1892, following an agreement between potential golfers and Penn Commoners for use of the Common. William Lloyd Roberts, landlord of the Barley Mow at the time was the first steward of the club, and the clubhouse was built next to the Barley Mow, being completed in 1900. It seems that the golfers did much to improve the state of the Common which had previously suffered from poor drainage, but disputes between the club and the commoners have arisen from time to time ever since. The 'Penn Artizans', however, still retain the right to play golf on the Common themselves and have their own clubhouse, also adjacent to the Barley Mow.

PENN CRICKET CLUB about the turn of the century.

PENN FIELDS HOCKEY CLUB in 1900. The team, which had its ground in Coalway Lane played in black shorts and shirts with white collars, and its captain was a Wolverhampton solicitor, F.H. Whitehouse. The annual subscription was a guinea.

PLAYING BOWLS AT BRADMORE RECREATION GROUND in the 1960s. St Philip's church can just be seen in the background.

THIS PHOTOGRAPH probably shows members of Penn Cycling Club at about the turn of the century, although it is not firmly identified. Note the bugle lying on the grass in the bottom right-hand corner.

THE PENN AMATEUR DRAMATIC SOCIETY pictured in the Church Room in the 1930s. Among those in the photograph are Eunice and Roger Piper, Mrs Tom Roden, Margaret and Floss Hickman, Mr and Mrs Wright of Church Hill, Harold Pinney, Maisie and Jack Webster and Mr and Mrs Percival.

THE MERRY HILL in 1931, soon after opening. It is interesting that this publicity photograph shows women enjoying a drink on their own.

THE ROEBUCK INN, just after it had been rebuilt. The half-demolished building in the foreground is the remains of the old pub.

THE VE DAY STREET PARTY in Cardiff Street, Penn Fields in 1945.

TWO PHOTOGRAPHS OF THE PENN PACK OF WOLF CUBS in the 1950s, on the right on an outing to Llandudno.

PENN CINEMA, WARSTONES ROAD, from the souvenir brochure issued at the opening on 27 December 1937 when the film shown was the Marx Brothers' *A Day at the Races*. The cinema was owned by B.T. Davis, a Birmingham accountant, and a consortium of local people, and was always popular in the locality. It was one of the last of the independent cinemas to close, showing its last film in March 1973. The site is now occupied by a supermarket.

At School in Penn

THE ORIGINAL ST BARTHOLOMEW'S SCHOOL, built about 1853 as a Sunday school. The day school moved to this site from Spring Hill in 1871.

ST BARTHOLOMEW'S SCHOOL PUPILS. Pictured on the left is Charles Henry Cole-Webb, vicar of Penn from 1883 to 1906, while the schoolmaster was Mr Holland.

ST BARTHOLOMEW'S SENIOR GIRLS' NETBALL TEAM in 1928.

ST BARTHOLOMEW'S SCHOOL GROUP pictured on the Common in about 1950.

ST BARTHOLOMEW'S FOOTBALL TEAM in 1952. Pictured in the back row are Mr Wilks, Michael Coley, David Pope, Keith Short, Edgar Hastings, David Robinson, John Crane and Geoffrey Hughes. In the middle row are Robert Scriven, Michael Welsbury, John Scriven, David Illage and Shaun Cook; while in the front row are John Whitehouse, Donald Smith, Brian Groves and Roger Hickman.

ST BARTHOLOMEW'S SENIOR GIRLS' NETBALL TEAM in 1952. Pictured in the back row are Miss Packham, Jean Holden, Ann Beddows, Shirley Reed, Elaine Marshall; and in front, Glenda Davis, Miriam Rollaston, Pauline Bailey, Carole Powell and Pat Davis.

WYNN'S SCHOOL c. 1899. This was the first school in Penn, having been built in 1714 from funds left by Charles Wynn, vicar of Penn from 1646 to 1669. It was situated at Springhill where Wynn's Crescent now runs, a spot which was thought convenient for children from both Upper and Lower Penn. By 1871 it was too small to accommodate all the children and the school moved temporarily to the St Bartholomew's Sunday school building while the Springhill school was enlarged.

PUPILS AT WOODFIELD AVENUE SCHOOL in 1916. The school had opened in 1913, supplementing the St Philip's National School near the church which had become too small for the children of the neighbourhood and could not find the money for extensions. Woodfield Avenue was a Board School.

WOODFIELD AVENUE SCHOOL CHOIR in the 1920s. Mr Brodie the headmaster was a former Wolves player.

A GIRLS' HANDIWORK CLASS outdoors at Woodfield Avenue School in 1923.

GIRLS FROM WOODFIELD AVENUE JUNIOR SCHOOL at camp at Enville in 1924.

THE ROYAL ORPHANAGE, PENN ROAD, which was founded in 1850 by local philanthropist John Lees as the Wolverhampton Orphan Asylum for children left orphaned by the cholera epidemic the previous year. The original institution was in Queen Street, Wolverhampton but the Penn Road site was purchased in 1852 and the new building opened in 1854. The orphanage became 'royal' in 1900 when it received a visit from the Duke and Duchess of York, the future King George V and Queen Mary. In 1944 it became the Royal Wolverhampton School. This photograph was taken after 1902 when the clock tower was installed to commemorate the coronation of Edward VII.

BOYS AND GIRLS OF THE ROYAL ORPHANAGE in the 1920s. The uniform was based on that of the Blue Coat School in London and was not changed to a more standard school uniform until after the Second World War.

GIRLS OF THE ROYAL ORPHANAGE in their distinctive uniforms playing with skipping ropes and other games at about the turn of the century.

The Religious Life

ST BARTHOLOMEW'S CHURCH around the turn of the century. The church was originally built in about 1200 by Sir Hugh de Bushbury, supposedly as an act of penance for killing a man in a quarrel. The tower dates from a major restoration carried out in 1764–5, and little of the church that existed before this date now survives. The chancel was rebuilt in 1871 and the nave extended at the same time. The church clock was given in 1887 to commemorate Queen Victoria's Jubilee.

ST BARTHOLOMEW'S CHURCH framed by trees. The setting of the church is still pleasantly rural in spite of the number of houses built in the vicinity in recent years. It is now within a conservation area.

ST BARTHOLOMEW'S CHURCH CHOIR in about 1925.

THE REMAINS OF THE SAXON CROSS in the churchyard at St Bartholomew's. This is known as Lady Godiva's Cross after the famous lady who is known to have owned parts of Penn before the Norman Conquest. Her son Aelfgar was also a local landowner.

LAYING THE FOUNDATION STONE for the organ loft at St Bartholomew's in 1901.

GALA DAY AT ST BARTHOLOMEW'S CHURCH, 15 September 1945. Pictured in the back row are Mr Shelley, headmaster of the school; Mr Folkes, churchwarden; Mrs Chester; Mrs Foote; Mrs Philip Hartill and Revd E. Hartill, while seated are the vicar's grandchildren, Mrs Beatrice Twentyman, and Mrs Hartill.

LOOKING FROM ST BARTHOLOMEW'S CHURCHYARD to the Church Room, opened in 1913. The base of the cross was probably the base of the sundial that had been made in 1682 by upturning the Norman font, now restored to its proper position inside the church. The cross itself was erected by Mrs A.C. Twentyman.

ROBERT LITTLEWOOD, organist and choirmaster at Penn parish church, pictured in 1941. Mr Littlewood was also the first conductor of the Penn Choral Society, founded in 1947.

A SERVICE WAS HELD to celebrate the 750th anniversary of St Bartholomew's church in 1950. Among those pictured are Revd Hartill, the vicar; Revd Shone, curate; Jack Tompkins and Mr Taylor, churchwardens; Tom Hinsall, verger; the Mayor and Mayoress of Wolverhampton and Mr and Mrs Ronald Sankey. The service was conducted by Bishop Woods of Lichfield.

REVD WILLIAM DALTON OF THE LLOYD. Born in Ireland, Dalton originally came to Wolverhampton to preach at St George's church but married Sarah Marsh, the wealthy widow of Richard Bayley Marsh of the Lloyd. Dalton was at that time working in Liverpool but his wife built him a new church, St Paul's, in Wolverhampton, to enable him to move to the town. He and his wife took a prominent part in the life of the town, building more churches and taking part in charitable works including the orphanage and the St Paul's Provident Society. Dalton was also a prolific writer of books and pamphlets. He died in 1880.

ST PHILIP'S CHURCH, PENN FIELDS, which was consecrated in 1859. The site was given by W.H. Sparrow of Penn Court in order to build a new church for the growing population of this area. At first it was a chapelry of St Bartholomew's with Reverend Dalton of Lloyd House as curate, but it became an independent parish in 1880. At first the church was probably lit by oil lamps, but gas lighting had been installed by 1895, causing an explosion and fire soon afterwards.

"StoneLaying"

St Chad's Ch Wolverhampton. Jan 25 1908

LAYING THE FOUNDATION STONE of St Chad's church, Owen Road, 25 January 1908. After a parade from the old mission church, the ceremony was performed by the Hon. Mrs Augustus Legge, wife of the Bishop of Lichfield. The church, which cost £5,000, was designed by local architect F.T. Beck and built by Henry Lovatt.

THE INTERIOR OF ST CHAD'S CHURCH, which is now used as a community centre and sports hall.

LEA ROAD CONGREGATIONAL CHURCH in about 1932 soon after its opening. The opening ceremony on 7 March 1932 was performed by Mrs James Thompson of Ludstone Hall, Claverley, and the service was conducted by Revd S.M. Berry, secretary of the Congregational Union of England and Wales, and son of Dr Charles Berry, the famous Wolverhampton writer and preacher.

SWAN BANK CONGREGATIONAL CHURCH, opened in 1902. In 1966 the congregation of this church combined with the Penn Congregational church which was renamed the Penn United Reformed Church in 1972.

PENN UNITED REFORMED CHURCH in course of building in 1951.

THE OPENING OF THE NEW BRADMORE METHODIST CHAPEL in 1907. This chapel had begun as a cottage meeting organized by Penn Road church from 1883 onwards. It closed in the 1920s when the congregation amalgamated with Penn Road to found the new Beckminster church.

BRADMORE SUNDAY SCHOOL ANNIVERSARY, 1908.

THE BRADMORE METHODIST CHAPEL MOTHERS MEETING on an outing to the Wrekin in about 1910.

THE OLD BRADMORE METHODIST CHAPEL in 1899. This was located in a disused smithy on the site of the Bradmore Arms and was opened on 25 April 1899. Eventually the congregation purchased land on the opposite corner of Birches Barn Road and opened a new chapel in 1907.

LAYING THE FOUNDATION STONE of Beckminster Methodist Church, 9 July 1925.

BECKMINSTER METHODIST CHURCH soon after its opening on 10 June 1926. The church was formed by the coming together of the Penn Road and Bradmore chapels which subsequently closed. Beckminster is now at the head of the Trinity Methodist Circuit.

ACKNOWLEDGEMENTS

Wolverhampton Public Libraries and the author are most grateful to everyone who has loaned or donated local photographs to their collections, either in the past or specially for this book. The author particularly acknowledges the help of the following for contributing pictures and information for *Penn in Old Photographs*. Without their assistance the compilation of the book would have been impossible.

Mr & Mrs Lawson Cartwright • Miss A. Price • Mrs D. Bodman
Mr & Mrs Jones • Mr Alex Chatwin • Mr Ned Williams • Mr J.L. Davies
Mr Collins • Mr Angus Dunphy • Mr Wheeler • Mrs M. Roper • Mrs J. Turner
Mrs Powell • Mr & Mrs Redfern • St Bartholomew's church and its members
Beckminster Methodist church and its members • Mitchell & Butler.